WALKING IN MY TRUTH

Table of Contents

PRAYER	3
STRATGY	5
PUBLIC LYNCHING	6
ACKNOWLEDGE US	8
EXHALE	11
TIME STAND STILL	13
UNFLAWED BEAUTY	15
UNCONDITIONAL LOVE	17
MENTAL INTERLUDE	19
VERBAL INTERCOURSE	21
CLIMAX	23
UNKNOWN LUMINARY	25
THE COMFORTABLE STRANGER	27
IT'S JUST A…	30
YOU THINK YOU'RE SO SEXY	32
SIDE CHICK	35
HIM	37
TO KNOW ME	39
WHO AM I RUNNING FROM?	40
PAIN	42
NO ONE'S INTERSTED IN THE TRUTH	44
REFUSAL	45
MEANS OF SURVIVAL	46
THE REAL ME	47
POWERLESS	50
OVERDUE CONVERSATION	51
AM I THE ONLY ONE?	52
I MOTHERFUCKING PINKY SWEAR	54
INSANE	56
VERBIAGE	58
WORDSMIFF	59
TRIBUTE	62

PRAYER

I know I haven't been the best of your servants

And at times I stray from your path more often than you would want me to.

And then there are those times I get so wrapped up in what's going on around me that I sometimes forget to keep you first even though you have yet to forget about me.

And sometimes I journey down roads not knowing where they lead not knowing what's waiting at the road's ends, but no matter what you have always been there to lead me through the shadows of darkness.

You have always been there to pick me up when I have fallen or when I have been knocked down and stepped upon.

You have always shown me empathy and not apathy.

You have always been most merciful when I couldn't be merciful with myself.

You have always been so extremely forgiving of me and my sins even when I couldn't find it in my heart to forgive myself.

I thank you for allowing me to breathe another breath of fresh air.

I thank you for giving me a chance to live this precious life you have granted me.

And just as Langston Hughes my life hasn't exactly been a crystal stair, for without a doubt I've had many trials, tribulations, problems, and issues but it is a life that I shall not take for granted.

Amen.

WALKING IN MY TRUTH

STRATEGY

They tried to cover us but didn't know in our pockets were seeds

We burst through the concrete like those can't kill weeds

We'll hear the dog whistle when it's time to strike

The revolution won't be televised but you'll hear the words through a mic

Chess strategy is the reality to protect the king

A power struggle between the two but out of control you are spiraling

Preparation for annihilation is the key to survival

Half of the country is insane while the other half is suicidal

PUBLIC LYNCHING

There will be a public lynching today. The way it was many years ago, people sitting on lawns, eating watercress sandwiches while someone's child swung from a tree.

Mass cranial incarceration has replaced the shackles and chains.

Too many are more concerned with performing or receiving brains.

History is repeating itself guess memories are a little hazy

Political incorrectness has nothing on the vernacular spewed on a daily

Voices are loud and overbearing so it's time to fight right

Culture has been appropriated, subjugated, emasculated, and back living in apartheid

Might as well he homeless, destitute, and intellectually corrupt

Financially unmotivated and morally bankrupt

Grabbing pussies by a bunch of pussies they all are a bunch of dicks

Your eyes are lying listen to these politricks

Turn back the hands of time to public lynchings

Better open that third eye and stop that dry snitching

WALKING IN MY TRUTH

There will be a public lynching today or at least there's supposed to be. The revolution began without the knowledge of the masses. Most are blind some are still sleep. Remember strength in numbers don't forget to prop up the weak. There's supposed to be a public lynching, but yeah today is not that day.

ACKNOWLEDGE US

The media is a part of the trouble

No one acknowledges the struggle

They allow the minority vultures

To define the majority of our culture

Black lives matter but only to a few

There's video of murders benefit of the doubt goes to the boys in blue

And don't give me that bullshit about black on black crime

My ancestors have been dying by your hands for a very long time

Black boys and girls are placed in special education

But that's only because you have high hopes of your culture's proliferation

The 13th amendment was abolished except for those imprisoned

Lies and deceit have a race of people culturally conditioned

Asleep at the wheel believing anything that's said

So much agony so much bloodshed

It's a war among each other but there has to unity

WALKING IN MY TRUTH

This is after all home of the free and the land of opportunity

Need to think like Martin have that Malcolm fight

Organize like Fred and never give up your rights

Lay our life on line for a country that doesn't love us back

Or only love us when we have a ball in our hand what kind of shit is that

Defend that flag at all cost but you have to admit the anthem is racist

Everything is cool as long as we know where our place is

Reverse racism is a made up construct just to distract

From the real racism that's inflicted upon blacks

You know its white privilege when equality feels like oppression

And you think you are being punished when someone else gets a blessing

We're all created equal but our burden is a little heavier our road a little longer

But taking a stand for what you believe in don't make you righter while taking a knee don't make me wronger

But you don't like how I protest but it's my right it's in the constitution

WALKING IN MY TRUTH

As a matter of fact, you don't like any of my solutions

Hands up don't shoot, black lives matter protest and marches

These events wouldn't occur if our punishments weren't the harshest

Riddle melanated communities with guns and drugs

Take the black man out of the home and then say the community is fucked up

You want an entire community dependent on the government

But most didn't want their help so you misrepresented

Skewed public perception to who were the real recipients

But you wanted everyone to stay in a state of oblivion

And let's not forget those that look like us that act like Uncle Ruckus

Can hardly wait drop a dime because they don't fuck with us

But the media is only part of the problem the rest lay at our feet

Are you going to stand tall with your fist raise or bow to the man under the sheet?

WALKING IN MY TRUTH

EXHALE

As the sun shines down upon my pale skin I sit and wonder what's to come

I met you and never fathom that I would grow to like you as much as I do

The way you look into my eyes and say nothing but an entire conversation is held

The way you sense my mood changes without me saying a word

The way you hold me when I need comfort or while I sleep

It's amazing how hearing you breathe makes me feel so at ease

My heart doesn't flutter at the sight of you and I'm not all giddy at the sound of your voice

The time that you have been a part of my life has been so exuberating

I've never smiled as much as I do since you've entered my life

WALKING IN MY TRUTH

You have brought back happiness to a life that once only knew despair

You have washed away the tears and turned my grey skies blue once again

And you, my love is one of the major reasons I continue to smile

Now I can truly exhale.

TIME STAND STILL

Time certainly has stood still for you, but me like the sands of an hourglass.

Don't get me wrong, it's nice to see you but what you want I cannot accommodate.

You have to realize that my life isn't a revolving door just for your convenience.

My life is like a club, once you leave you must pay to re-enter.

I apologize for being so blunt, no not really, but that's how you made it.

All the cheating, all the lies, all the deceit, you actually thought I wasn't going to find out about all your misdeeds.

I mean I loved you. I gave up a lot not only for you but in spite of you and what did you do? What did you give up? Nothing! You used me! As if I was your own personal whore.

Yes, I chuckle a little, it's a tad funny because I must admit at first I was a little irate with you. But when I realized what you did for me rather than to me there was no way for me to be infuriated. Your infidelity and disrespect made me realize that I didn't need you to complete me.

You weren't an entire entity yourself so how could you complete me.

You made me realize that I was a filler for your abyss of uncertainty and emotions, when you degraded me and mentally abused me.

All you did was give me the strength to move on. And move on I sure did.

Yes, time has stood still for you.

But while you kept that underdeveloped prepubescent mind state, I grew into something you will never be able to handle...

A beautiful woman.

UNFLAWED BEAUTY

Do I really have to struggle?

Like I really have a choice

I make my opinion heard

But you're not hearing my voice

You try to degrade me

But you can't break my spirit

My skin has melanin

And proudly I'll wear it.

Black is not only beautiful

But it has a royal status

The ill words you speak to me

Don't really matter

You can call me a spook

A coon, a nigger

But I'm getting my education to take your job

And clock those major figures

My folks can do more than just

Chill on the corner and smoke out

I'm a part of a darker breed

WALKING IN MY TRUTH

You don't know what the 3rd eye is about

You sit and sometimes pray

Wanting me to commit genocide

But Imma love my brothers and sisters

Until my untimely demise

I'm going to uplift my people

Because that is my duty

When I look in the mirror

All I see is unflawed beauty

UNCONDITIONAL LOVE

There comes a time in everyone's life that we all must face some vast realities

There have been misconceptions that we have been a part of and misinterpretations that we have created,

But eventually we've all had to find it in our heart to forgive and embrace those that have wronged us.

I never asked anyone to cater to my every beck and call.

I never tried to hide my imperfections or pretended to be what I am not.

I do; however, want everyone to accept me for who I am, flaws and all.

You want to accept me only on your terms,

There was no offer of compromise or invitations to meet me halfway.

I'm at a point in my life where everything matters and yet nothing matters at all

All words that left your mouth was full of lies and deceit

A thought of me lying to you left me with a feeling of guilt, but I continued to stand by you.

WALKING IN MY TRUTH

Your love for me came with stipulations and conditions

I loved you unconditionally every minute of every day and I continued to be the support when you needed it.

To me that's unconditional love

Now tell me what does it mean to you?

MENTAL INTERLUDE

Stimulation of the mind, a new form of oral sex

Ideas emitted from your ear trickling down your neck

Impregnating your mind with my verbal ejaculation

Reproducing knowledge in the form of masturbation

Having verbal intercourse that cause neurological orgasms

That sends your entire body in a biological spasm

Allow me to penetrate your cranium with my erect thoughts

While ovulating all theorems from which I've been taught

Permit me to flow through your mind just like menstruation

As I develop your intellect and shower it with fertilization

Can I stimulate your brain and evaluate your mental capacity?

While our genes intertwine causing major catastrophes

Basking in the afterglow of the climax just reached

I am now the student it's your turn to teach

WALKING IN MY TRUTH

As you enter my sacred temple stroking my thought process

It's your mind I inspire to capture and your body I want to caress

Join me with your knowledge this world we will elude free

your mind, relax your soul with my mental interlude.

VERBAL INTERCOURSE

I need that verbal intercourse

That mental masturbation

That mind altering feeling

That lay on my back sensation

I need that climax after the after glow

After the climax that I have reached

I need you to have me stumbling around

Mixing up all parts of speech

I need to have that fog in my head

The light shining from my eye

I need you to have me questioning everything

I need you to have me wanting to cry

Bend my mind, I get twisted like the exorcist

I make you sweat while I just mist

I want to hit octaves that opera hasn't heard

Got me all geeked like I'm some kind of nerd

I'm as giddy as a kid sitting in the candy aisle

WALKING IN MY TRUTH

Let me finish dropping knowledge

It's flowing like the Nile

It'll never dry up, it'll always be moist

Come on give me that verbal intercourse.

CLIMAX

There should be a very definitive answer to how does climax feel to you but for me it's never that simple. How climax feels to me all depends on whether I'm present and participating or if I'm just going through the motions.

If I'm just going through the motions, while I'm physically there emotionally and mentally I'm not. Why am I engaging, probably to kill time or was I bored. More than likely they didn't connect with me mentally and I needed an itch scratched but in the process I detached mentally and emotionally.

However, if I'm present and participating the climax starts from the first kiss. It feels like a burning ember in the pit of my stomach. His hands caressing my breasts and massaging my torso, while warming my inner spirit. His kisses on my back and butt sends chills though my body. And by the time he enters my temple I'm ready to receive his goodness. The moans, the pleasurable *ahhhhs*, the slow and steady rhythmic motion wells that climatic feeling even more. His arms around me as I ride him and his whispers telling me he wants me to climax with him along with his soft lips on my breast. And when I'm ready he flips me and his rhythm picks up. I softly whisper faster and harder between moans of pleasure. And when I feel him ready to explode I feel this indescribable feeling take over my entire body. Our bodies in opposition of each while being entwined with each other. Perspiration dripping, pores open, not wanting to be touched but not wanting to let go. Having the desire to continue but knowing you can't because with every subsequent touch your body goes into uncontrollable convulsions, and while he offers oral stimulation you turn him down because there's nothing like climaxing from him being inside your temple.

UNKNOWN LUMINARY

He said he'll always be there for you

But you took that with a grain of salt

You had people tell you that all your life and you still felt like everything was

all your fault

But he was there every time you needed someone

He was there ready to wrap his arms around you and take the pain away

You felt the protection he told you he would always provide for you

And for the first time in a long time

You felt safe

You felt secure

Every time you needed him he was there

He didn't want anything in return but your love

In some aspects you didn't really know how to react to that

You've been loved before unequivocally and without restriction

And you thrived but this right here has been over 20 years in the making

WALKING IN MY TRUTH

He's not afraid of adversity

He's not going to run at the first sign of dismay

He's buckling down with you and he's going to guide you

through this storm

called life

Isn't that what you want

Better yet that's what you need

You know a king when you see one

You know with him you can be submissive

With him you know you won't be lead astray

A few years ago you didn't think you'd be here again

But he's the first person you think about when your day begins

And the last person you say good night to

He's the first person you want to share your joys with and the

last person you

want to disappoint

You know he's your king but you just hope that you measure up

to be the queen he deserves.

THE COMFORTABLE STRANGER

He greeted me with a hello.

His welcoming eyes let me know that just as I was excited for his presence he was just as excited to be there.

We gave each other the customary socially accepted hug.

He said "Don't look, I need to prepare."

So I averted my eyes just to make him feel better.

He disappeared and I went back to lounging.

While he was a stranger to me I was comfortable with him being in my space.

He was the comfortable stranger.

There's something sexy about a man that walks with an air of confidence.

Not too arrogant but still confident enough to navigate through life.

This encompasses the comfortable stranger perfectly.

He emerges and rest next to me without saying a word.

It's a bit funny because it seems as if he's a school boy who was shy and didn't know what to say.

He finally touched me and told me to turn over.

He starts massaging my back and

I think, "How did he know I needed one of these?"

He was caught off guard because I was bottomless,

But he continues without missing a beat.

He tells me that I'm tense, my response "It's been a long time and I'm extremely stressed".

He continues moving his fingers up and down my back.

The feeling of those strong hands caressing a portion of my body helped relax me even more.

Our idle conversation is unmemorable and mostly incoherent but it was perfect for the moment with the comfortable stranger.

He turned me over, rubbing and massaging the front of my body

He began by kissing my forehead before moving to my neck.

He caressed and kissed my bosom, lingering there because he's been told I like that.

He knew he was there for one reason but he didn't want to stick and move.

He wanted to no longer be the comfortable stranger but soon realized that's all he could be.

Finally, the *ahhhhs* filled the room.

And so did the grasping of the sheets and the scratching of the back.

The movements and rhythm while not on beat with the music that was on Pandora but was in tune with the music that he and I were making as we waltzed and salsaed.

We were met with the sun rising while we still danced throughout the night.

The *ahhhhs* still filled the room.

Then there was an explosion of pleasure.

The comfortable stranger and I collapsed from exhaustion.

All of the dancing finally caught up with us.

The conversation was still unmemorable.

Even though I was breaking all the rules I will never forget the comfortable stranger.

IT'S JUST A ...

It's just a dick...no it's not

It is the means of oppression

It is the tool used to rape and pillage

The souls and innocence of many.

It's just a dick...no it's not

It's the means of reproduction

It's used to fertilize the seeds

That rest in the womb

It's just a dick...no it's not

While it can be used to inflict pain

It is also used to provide sheer pleasure

It's only a dick...no it's not

It is what identifies you as male

It's what keep women earning less

For doing the same job

It's only a dick...no it's not

It's the ying to my yang

WALKING IN MY TRUTH

It's the sun to my moon

It's the king to my queen

But for you it can remain just a dick

YOU THINK YOU'RE SO SEXY

You walk around with pep in your step like you just won a multimillion dollar lottery. Don't get me wrong, I love a man with confidence but you … you are a half step to the left to just being an asshole. But here's what you need to know about me. I'm not impressed by material items, I'm not impressed by the clothes and shoes you wear. Or what type of car that you drive. And despite my look of interest, I'm not that impressed by you reliving your young adult life through you retelling the same stories over and over again. I get it, you are smart and intelligent, you served your country where you consistently got in trouble, and you can hold a conversation about life in general. Bravo! So when we get together to exchange fuck faces all that tryna be sexy and tryna look sexy is waaaaaay over the top. I'm not interested in your pseudo-seductive looks while you struggle with your rhythm. And please don't think because you have a penis it means it is to go in my mouth. Yes, I know I'm selfish, but I didn't ask you to kiss my second pair of lips. As a matter of fact, I told you I didn't want you to and you got mad. I truly tried to help you out by telling you what I like so we can avoid that whole trial and error awkward moment but you said I was too demanding. Apparently I'm not supposed have a say in my pleasure, Negro please. I've been responsible for my own orgasm for a long time.

I enjoyed talking to you. You know those happy hours we spent chatting it up. Those times you thought you were sizing me up and grooming me to make that smooth move that you use on other women to get them in bed. Yeah while it seemed it worked it really didn't, because after about 10 minutes of hanging out with everyone that first time, I already knew we'd end up fucking. What you didn't know was once I got the drawls, any intellectual attraction was gone. No emotions, no lying around in bed talking, no staying the night. The agenda goes… you come, you cum, you go the hell home. I know it's a bit brash but let's keep it real, you are otherwise attached. You aren't making any moves to change that, so don't think I'm going to give you husband privileges while you are just on fuck face exchange status.

SIDE CHICK

I'm not the side chick or the other woman, I have to be the only. I need all the attention. I need to be first. I need you to come over when I need you. I need to see you when I want to see you. I need you to hold me when I can't sleep at night. I need you to wipe away my tears when my anxiety rears its ugly head. I need to feel that cover of protection. I need to feel secure in knowing that you are there no matter what even if you are not there physically. You said you love me but you aren't the man to fill my needs. And I appreciate that honesty. But yet and still you come to me with and for kisses and sex. You know I'm missing that in my life and you are more than happy to fulfill that need. And I'm more than willing to let you. And just as much as I want it you aren't fulfilling the need. You can't give me what I want — no you can't give me what I need when I want it. And trust I want it all the time. You slid through and you got your nut and I'm still feeling unfulfilled.

You want to know why I don't just cavalierly suck dick? It's because I don't like to suck anyone's dick that's not lying next to me every night. The truth is, not only are my skills in the bed on point but my oral skills are as well. Something you may never know about.

Do I love you? I don't know if I love you but I won't let myself venture down that road. I don't want to get hurt. I can't allow myself to get hurt. I can't take another disappointment. And I can't be your side chick anymore.

HIM

I always felt that I needed him.

He was my essence, my heart, my everything.

Everything I never knew I always wanted.

Now to see him arm in arm with another broad

Doesn't hurt as much as I thought.

Yes, I still care. Yes, love is still there,

But not in a sense of me loving him more than I love myself.

I always felt I needed him.

Even on that day that he walked into my life just to tell me he

was walking out of my life

And all I could say was…

Okay!

I didn't yell or scream

You see I never was in the business to keep someone who didn't

want to be kept.

He wiggled to get loose and I loosened my grasp,

He slid from my fingers and backed away while telling me he

was sorry how he never meant to hurt me and how good I was

to him (you damn right I treated him like a fucking king).

But he still left!

I always felt I needed him

To lean on, on those days that I needed a good cry, a shoulder to rest my head upon, or a sounding board.

He was my best friend, my everything, my essence, my reason for being.

But with him gone living a carefree life as if I never existed, I realized

I wanted him, I always needed me.

While there is still residual love for him, there is an unwavering unbreakable love for me, and that's all I ever needed.

TO KNOW ME

To know me with your eyes and judge me with your mind

Isn't the same as knowing me with your heart

To know me is to know things you can't possibly fathom

To know me is to know why the sky is blue or why water is wet

Things that mystify the world

To know me is to know why we've been plagued with incurable diseases

To know me is to know why so much animosity is between two people of the

same likeness

To know me is to know why someone is born homo, bi, or heterosexual

To know me is to know that at any given time your worst nightmare can

become your reality

And you still want to know me?

WHO AM I RUNNING FROM?

Shadows lurk in alleys

Waiting for me to appear

I walk, I run, I try to ignore

The deep inset fear

Silhouettes I notice around

I wonder who's behind the form

These shadows that remain lurking

Seem to be full of nothing but scorn

At night I toss and turn

These shadows are in my dreams

Darkness fill my night

And no one can help it seems

I'm constantly running away

From someone I don't know who

I'm always walking on egg shells

I want to start my life anew

But the continuous running and hiding

That's something I cannot do

Please look into my eyes

WALKING IN MY TRUTH

Tell me you see them too

Many days I sit and wonder

Where I'm going and from where I've come

But first I need to figure out

Who I'm running from?

WALKING IN MY TRUTH

Pain

I feel the pain you feel. The tears that ran down my cheeks are your tears. The pain I feel in my eyes from crying is the pain you felt. The tightness I feel in my chest is the tightness you felt as you sobbed. I'm here. I acknowledge your pain, I acknowledge your trauma. No more walls. Don't shut me out. You are so beautiful and you don't even know it. You have endured so much but your spirit--- words cannot express what I see in your spirit. I sat and cried with you during every word. You reminded me of everything that I buried. You reminded me of how much you no longer wanted to continue to live. But you reminded me of how tenacious and determined you were to continue despite not wanting to live. It's you that I draw my strength. Your compassion for others is unlike any other I have ever encountered. You make sacrifices for others when you don't necessarily have to, and you never ask for anything in return. You see and hear the beauty in objects and people that others don't see or hear. You aren't easily intimidated. You will stand up for everything you believe in no matter how frightening it is.

You try to make sure, everyone around you is tension free. You are a natural comedienne. You can make someone who is having a lousy day brighter with just conversation. They think its jokes but you are speaking about life. You have such a beautiful aura about you. A ring of positivity that stays with you always, even when you aren't positive about yourself. And when you love, you love so hard. You love with every fiber of your being. But make no mistake your cut off game is serious. You are the one that deserves all the praise for why I am where I am today. Considering everything that has happened to you, you persevered, you overcame, you rocked the hell out of life and you made it so look easy. No one can ever take away any of your accomplishments.

None of these accomplishments may get the acknowledgment that they rightly deserve but I acknowledge each and every one of them because without them there would be no me. I love you for all your flaws and imperfections. I hate everything you went through as a young girl but the result of those flaws and imperfections is the woman I have become.

NO ONE'S INTERESTED IN THE TRUTH

Are you planning on hurting yourself?

Only on the inside.

Sitting quietly holding everything in,

Not wanting to bother anyone with the troubles I hide.

It seems as if no one will understand or care to listen.

I don't want to bother anyone because they're traveling their

own life's mission.

People ask how you are doing but they really don't care to know.

They want the socially accepted answers of great or fine.

But if you tell them the truth that you have aches and pains or

you are depressed they sit in silences as if they are a mime.

So I give them

What they expect since they really don't care any way

They just proclaim they do as it's something nice to say.

REFUSAL

No one ever heard my silent screams

Or ever supported my higher dreams

No one ever saw all my pain

No one ever covered me from the rain

I felt I had no will to live

But I only have one life to give

I live my life still depressed

I do my best to stay less stressed

My thoughts are scattered with random thoughts

I refuse to be another black girl lost

MEANS OF SURVIVAL

I have a lot of thoughts but none are suicidal

I never put my faith in any false idol

Music and poetry are my means of survival

I took out my bible put it on vinyl now I am a disciple

I use spoken word performances as my revival

I put my pen to paper to capture my arrival

THE REAL ME

You want me to keep it one hunnit

Well, I can't.

You see I don't know the real me.

The real me was lost years ago.

I am only a facsimile of who I was supposed to be.

The person I was supposed to be was stripped from me.

Just like my innocence.

You see the real me was raped.

The real me was threatened.

The real me was forced to commit sexual acts that a child

shouldn't even know what they are.

You want me to keep it one hunnit.

Sure.

I don't know who I am or who I was supposed to be.

I can only tell you what my dreams were.

I can only tell you how I circumvented the reality that could

have destroyed my life.

I can tell you how my altered childhood made me into who I am

today.

WALKING IN MY TRUTH

But you don't want to hear about that.

No one wants to hear about that.

You see misery loves company and it also garners attention.

I don't want that type of company nor do I want any attention.

Actually I try to stay out of anyone's spotlight.

I don't want your sympathy or your empathy.

I never wanted to be angry and not trusting. All I ever wanted was to just be me.

You want to know who I am.

I am a scared little girl in a world that I shouldn't be in.

I'm an angry child that is full of sin.

I'm a little girl that never told.

And that same little girl whose soul was sold.

I'm that little girl whose innocence was lost at four.

The little girl who is ashamed because she seemed to enjoy.

That little girl with numb feelings.

The little girl that needed healing.

I'm the little girl that was called weird and I just wanted to be alone.

The little girl that just wanted to right her wrong.

I'm the little girl that became an adult that didn't like to be touched but loved to be touch.

I'm that little girl that became an adult that was told that she wanted too much.

I'm that little girl that became an adult that just wanted intimacy.

Everyone wants me to tell them about the real me.

Just a cursory look into pain I've been through.

I told you about the real me now show me the real you.

POWERLESS

I sit powerless angry and confused

No amount of forgiveness can ever remove

The violation of space the attack on my being

This can't be reality I have to be dreaming

I'm a survivor but why do I have to be

I can't feel safe while walking down my street

I can't feel safe sitting in my own home

I can't feel safe in a crowd or alone

No one in my life has the benefit of the doubt

Everyone get one strike and they are out

I trust very few and is comfortable with even less

This is my reality, and every day I live with this mess.

But somehow I continue making the most of what I've been given

One day I'll take back the power of the powerless life I've been living.

OVERDUE CONVERSATION

Listen baby girl, I know that you are scared.

But believe me when I tell you there is nothing to fear.

I know I let you down in the past but I was younger then.

I put this on my life I'll never let it happen again

I hear your words but I've heard them before.

Every time I trusted I was betrayed for sure.

I put my faith in a false idol, prayed to an invisible being.

But like clockwork no one heard my silent screams.

I know I know and it hurts me cuz I know your pain

But it took me a lifetime to acknowledge that ball and chain.

But now that I have I can protect you from any danger

Just remember sometimes family is worse than a stranger.

But how can you protect me you couldn't earlier

I'm older and wiser but my vision isn't blurrier.

I know you are still scared but please trust me

I'll never let anyone else hurt you that I can guarantee.

WALKING IN MY TRUTH

AM I THE ONLY ONE?

Some days I feel awkward as hell

A fraud, weird, and out of place

Mixed in with the upper echelon of people

Who have a good grasp on life?

They know where they are going and how to get there.

Am I the only one? Am I the only one?

Am I the only one that wakes up in the middle of the night scared that my past is gaining on me?

Am I the only one that can hide in plain sight and be alone in a crowded room?

Am I the only one who feels they are being mentally held hostage and constantly fighting to be free?

Am I the only one who is the smartest in the room with the best idea that no one hears so the project will meet its doom?

Am I the only one who walks in my truth each and every day flaunting all of my flaws?

WALKING IN MY TRUTH

Am I the only one who realize that even when constantly sharpened, a pencil still writes when it's small?

Someday I feel out of place, a fraud, weird, and awkward as hell.

When around a bunch of other creatives, really how can anyone tell?

WALKING IN MY TRUTH

I MOTHERFUCKING PINKY SWEAR

I motherfucking pinky swear if I have another person ask me

how I'm doing

And give me the answer they want to hear I'm going to scream

The reality is they are living a lie being played out

In a messed-up dream

They don't know me and truthfully the don't want to

They want me to be the character in the play their brain has

going on

They don't want to acknowledge what's really going on

So, let me hip them to a few things that I've been going through

When I get overwhelmed I need to take a day or two

I was raped and sexually assaulted all before the age of five

And I wonder sometimes how I'm still alive

Before I was ten I thought I was pregnant by my rapist

There was nowhere for me to go to try to escape this

I learn to deal with it all by withdrawing inward

But staying to yourself isn't a good thing growing up in the

hood.

WALKING IN MY TRUTH

Back then kids didn't tell, our business was ours

But that rape and assault was about nothing but power

I grew up quick using writing and sex as my coping mechanism

Kept my head in books gaining more knowledge and wisdom

Not many knew that I was raped at a very young age

Not many knew that I was full of so much rage

Diagnosed with PTSD, anxiety and massive depressive disorder

But to hear some tell it all I needed was some holy water

Just go pray they would say, you don't pray enough

Yeah it was church people that put me in the situation that was tough

I'll take my chances with the devil, if that's your savior in action

But I can't go certain places, smell or see certain things without having an anxiety reaction

I motherfucking pinky swear if I ever see any of them again

I'll shake my head and walk away and let their God take care of them.

INSANE

Insanity blows my mind

As I press rewind

And peep you from behind

New daily complications

Of poetical impregnations

Flowing through the lips like lyrical abbreviations

Constant use of drugs

Self-proclamation of being thug

Caught in the crossfire, what the fuuuuuuuuck

Verbal detonation

Impromptu presentation

No blood or crip or any other gang affiliation

Asymmetric sounds

Parallel all around

Tell me how can I be down

Thought just flow from the pen to the pad

Verbiage used you wish you had

WALKING IN MY TRUTH

Like Michael Jackson said "I'm Bad"

Time stands still but eons past

Ego trips and spiritual fast

So put it in writing to make it last.

VERBIAGE

With proper speech and Ebonics dialect

A street smart style and academia intellect

Separating fallacies from present realities

Dissolve negative energy create positivity

Support the brothers help them to be strong

Be their central support system help them hold on

Aid today's youth while giving birth to a nation

Forget physical violence concentrate on mental recreation

Expound on ideas and creative aspects

Always know where to go but never know what to expect

To know what you're getting into you must know the past

Don't hide the indifference behind the native mask

Let's keep it real for all those concerned

If it's continuously taught eventually we'll learn

We have the mental capacity to conquer any war

As long as we keep it mentally challenging and intellectually

raw

WORDSMIFF

Although I walk through the valley of the shadow of death

The soul of my fire remains calm

True beauty is in the eye of the beholder

And I've written my own book of Psalms

Oh hear ye, hear ye, I'm back with my pen

My thoughts ricochet like bullets so I'm at it again

Regurgitating flow all over my paper

Like Nature's Fury I get away with my capers

That's who I am can't be nobody else

How conceited am I, I could kiss myself?

Mental Interludes and freaky satisfaction

Everything has an opposite yet an equal reaction

I'm like a chemical experiment blowing up in your face

I'm like a marathon runner you can't keep up with my pace

I change styles like a prostitute turn tricks

Watching you analyze me that's how I get my kicks

WALKING IN MY TRUTH

I have more game than all sports combined

And I'm so cute I look better than two dimes

I got more love than there was at the last supper

And I get around more often than a trucker

I have better aim than a guided missile

And I'm extremely rare like a diamond whistle

That's who I am can't be nobody else

How conceited am I, I could kiss myself?

I'll make you think deeper than there is outer space

Whether street or professional I can never be outta place

I have more darkness than 2 seconds after midnight

I have so much skillz if I was illiterate I could still write

That's who I am, can't be nobody else

How conceited am I, I could kiss myself?

I hear the amens and I hear ya's flowing from your lips

I's still shedding tears for my peoples on those ships

I'm hot like lava the mistress of my fate

You make me mad you just opened up hell's gate

WALKING IN MY TRUTH

I get slept on more than a worn out mattress

And my critics and haters will probably attack this.

Can't say that I blame them, I'd probably hate too

Cause I'm iller than AIDS mixed with the swine flu

But that's who I am, can't be nobody else

How conceited am I, I could kiss myself?

TRIBUTE

I remembered when I R&B'd and hip hopped my way to and through school

Never thinking I'd be standing here with you as my strength and counselor

I remember when I dismissed you as a mere fallacy that just invaded my space

Not knowing that the only fallacy I had was living without you

You have been my inspiration, a pillar of strength and knowledge.

It was you I spoke of in *Unflawed Beauty*, I just didn't know it.

I was you that rendered *Unconditional Love* to me I just didn't see it.

It was you that allowed me to express my emotions and discomfort without

fear of retribution or shame.

You encourage me to walk by faith and not by sight, while keeping my head up despite all that has gone wrong in my life.

You allowed me to be me and not a facsimile of what others thought I should be

WALKING IN MY TRUTH

You have been the level ground upon which I walk

You have been the silver lining of the clouds that my head is in

You have been patient with me when I couldn't even be patient with myself

You have held my hand and stood by me through my tribulations

You have helped me rise to the occasion when life has knocked me down

You did not allow me to give up when I was ready to say to hell with it and

throw in the towel

I received silent whispers from you when I needed them the most

You have shown me how to be a better mother, lover, daughter, sister,

confidant, and friend

And indeed, you have been one of my dearest and best friends

Because of you I will never put down my pen and I will never stop the flow

WALKING IN MY TRUTH

Of my *Mental Interludes*, I will never stop being a *Wordsmith*, I will never stop being me

As long as you continue being poetry.

www.ingramcontent.com/pod-product-compliance
Lightning Source LLC
Chambersburg PA
CBHW071756040426
42446CB00012B/2588